A Child's Story of Christmas

A CHILD'S STORY OF CHRISTMAS
adapted from
A CHILD'S LIFE OF JESUS
Copyright © 1951 by Fulton Oursler
Copyright © renewed 1978 by Fulton Oursler, Jr.,
Will Oursler, and April Armstrong.
Illustrations copyright © 1996 by Abingdon Press.
First Abingdon edition 1996.

This book is printed on recycled, acid-free paper.

ISBN 0-687-02200-2

96 97 98 99 00 01 02 03 04 — 10 9 8 7 6 5 4 3 2 1

Manufactured in Mexico

A Child's Story of Christmas

BY

Fulton Oursler

ILLUSTRATED BY HELEN CASWELL

Abingdon Press
Nashville

One winter's night, long, long ago, God, who made the moon and the rain and the rivers and the flowers and all the silvery stars and everything on the earth and in the sky, did a new and wonderful thing.

He sent his own dear Son down from Heaven to join the world and live with people like you and me for a while.

The Son of God did not come as a grown man at first. He was born as a tiny baby, like all the rest of us.

This is how it happened:

There lived in a little town called Nazareth a man and woman, named Joseph and Mary. One morning, when Mary was alone, an angel came into her kitchen and told her the big secret.

She was going to have a son, and God would be His Father. And the name of her son would be Jesus.

While Joseph lay asleep, the angel whispered the same secret to him.

So Mary and Joseph knew the greatest secret in the world.

The house where they lived in Nazareth had white walls and a round roof. It was a pretty house and Mary wanted her little boy to be born there. But Jesus was born far away from the pretty house with the white walls.

That was because the king of the land made everybody leave home and come to another town, where he could count the people and find out how many there were.

So Mary had to ride a long way on an old gray donkey while Joseph held the reins and walked beside her. Joseph was so tired that his feet hurt, and he and Mary could hardly keep awake when they got to the little town called Bethlehem.

Every hotel and rooming house and every inn was crowded. There was no room for Mary and Joseph at the inn or anywhere else, except a stable. A red cow lived in the stable and every once in a while said "moo." A black hen lived there, too, with a lot of yellow chicks and a donkey and a little white lamb with its mother.

Joseph found a corner in the stable and fixed a bed for Mary on the stable floor. Her bed was just a pile of warm straw, and Joseph rolled up his coat to be her pillow. She had no cradle for her little son, so she had to put him in a manger box full of hay for the donkey's breakfast.

And there the little Son of God opened His eyes for the first time.

Joseph thanked God for the wonderful gift of the little boy from Heaven. Joseph did not have a bed for himself. But he did not mind; he wanted to stay up all that first night and watch over the newborn baby and mother, while they were sleeping.

When everything was quiet, and only Joseph was awake, he heard a knock at the stable door. Some strange men were outside. They were shepherds who took care of flocks of sheep on the hillsides. They were tall, strong men with long staffs in their hands and their sun-burned faces and dark eyes were kind. All of them were breathing hard because they had run a long way and they were excited.

The shepherds told Joseph they wanted to come in to the stable.

"Why?" asked Joseph.

Then they told him what had happened. While they were watching their flocks of sheep they saw a bright-colored light fill the whole sky. Then they saw angels in the clouds and heard them singing:

"Glory to God . . ."

"And on earth, peace . . ."

One angel spoke to the shepherds:

"Great news. A Savior is born . . . Christ, the Lord."

The shepherds could hardly believe their ears. Christ was born! This was the first Christmas Day. And the angels told the shepherds that the little boy was in a stable not far away from them and their flocks of sheep, and that He was the Son of God.

This was great news. And the first to know it, outside of Mary and Joseph, were the shepherds, the poorest and gentlest of men. They were the first strangers to understand that the little Son of God was going to grow up and be a man and show people how to be kind and happy as God loves us all to be, before He would go home to His Father in Heaven.

Joseph told the shepherds the name of the baby. It was Jesus. The name Jesus means Savior. Jesus who was Christ the Lord came to the world to save all of us from our mistakes.

The shepherds wanted to see Jesus, so Joseph let them kneel down by the manger and look with wonder at the tiny baby lying asleep in the hay. And the shepherds thought:

"This is the most wonderful baby ever born. With Jesus the Son of God as a friend, no one will ever need to be afraid of anything again."

The shepherds laughed with joy, and hugged Joseph before they went back under the starry sky to tend their sheep.

Another night, Joseph heard three knocks at the door. Three kings from far away wanted to see Jesus, because they, too, knew that the little boy was the Son of God. They had come a long distance on camels because they had seen a great star in the East and followed it. They were sure the star would lead them to where the Savior of the world was born. And it did.

The kings brought presents for the newborn Jesus—sweet-smelling little boxes and a big bag of golden money—and gave them to Mary. Those were the very first Christmas gifts in the world.